MULTIPLE-CHOICE

ENGLISH

Practice Test 4

Guidance for completing this Test.

1. Read the passages carefully.

2. Read the questions thoroughly.

3. Read the answers carefully.

4. Choose what you think is the correct answer carefully.

5. Underline or circle the answer, immediately after the question.

6. Transfer the LETTER **A,B,C,D,E** or **N** to the answer sheet.

7. Make sure to mark the answer box like [—] not [╱].

8. Check carefully that you have transferred your correct answer.

9 . This test lasts for **50 minutes**.

PUPIL'S NAME _____

TOTAL MARK (Out of 60)	

Read this passage and answer the questions which follow. If there are any words you don't understand you may find them in the Glossary at the end of the test.

HIROSHIMA

1.   Before that morning in 1945 only a few conventional bombs, none of which did any great damage, had fallen on the city. Fleets of US bombers had, however, devastated many cities round about, and Hiroshima had begun a programme of evacuation of 250,000.

5.   Among the evacuees were Emiko and her family.

       They were moved out to Otake, a town about an hour's trainride out of the city. In 1945, Emiko had been a student, fragile and vivacious, versed in the gentle traditions of the tea ceremony and flower arrangement. Every day she and her sister Hideko used

10.   to travel into Hiroshima to school. Hideko had been thirteen, two years younger than Emiko. Their father was an antique dealer and he owned a house in the city, although it was empty now. Tetsuro, Emiko's fourteen year old brother was at the Manchurian front with the Japanese Imperial Army. Her mother was kept busy looking

15.   after the children, for her youngest daughter, Aiko, was sick with heart trouble and rations were scarce. All of the family were undernourished.

       On the night of August 5th, 1945, little Aiko was dangerously ill and was not expected to live. Everybody took turns

20.   watching by her bed, soothing her by massaging her arms and legs. Emiko went to bed at 8.30 and at midnight was awakened to take her turn with her sick sister. At 2.00 am she went back to sleep. While Emiko slept, the Enola Gay, a US B-29 bomber carrying the world's first operational atom bomb, was already in the air. She

25.   had taken off from the Pacific island of Iwo Jima at 1.45 am, and now Captain William Parsons, United States Navy ordnance expert was busy in the bomb-hold with the final assembly of Little Boy, the name of this devasting bomb. Little Boy looked much like an outsize T.N.T. blockbuster but the crew knew there was something different

30.   about it. Only Parsons and the pilot, Colonel Paul Tibbets, knew exactly in what manner Little Boy was different. The B-29 bomber and its lethal cargo of Little Boy was set for Hiroshima.
Emiko was still asleep.

       On board the Enola Gay co-pilot Captain Robert Lewis was

35.   writing up his personal log. "After leaving Iwo Jima," he recorded, "we began to pick up some low stratus cloud and before very long we were flying on top of an under-cast cloud. Apart from a thin high cirrus cloud and low stuff, it's a very beautiful day. "

Emiko and Hideko were up at six in the morning. They
40. dressed in the uniform of their women's college - white blouse,
quilted hat and black skirt - breakfasted and packed their
aluminium lunch-boxes with white rice and eggs. These they
stuffed into their shoulder bags as they hurried for the seven-o-clock
train to Hiroshima. Today there would be no classes as the
45. sisters were going to work on demolition, along with many
women's groups, high school students and others.

It was a lovely morning. While the two young girls were at
breakfast, Captain Lewis, while flying over the Pacific, made an
entry in his log book. "The bomb is now alive and it's a funny
50. feeling knowing it's right at the back of you. Touch wood !"

In the train Hideko and Emiko argued about their lunch. They
decided to meet at the main station that afternoon and catch the
five o'clock train home. By now they had arrived at the first of
Hiroshima's three stations.

**Answer the following questions. Look back over the passage.
You should choose the _best_ answer and mark its letter on
your answer sheet.**

1. How many people were to be evacuated from Hiroshima in
August 1945 ?

A. 400,000   B. 250,000
C. 150,000   D. 650,000
E. 1,000,000

2. When was little Aiko dangerously ill ?

A. 1.45 am   B. 8.30
C. 2.00 am   D. midnight
E. 5th August, 1945

3. What was the name of the co-pilot of the US B-29 bomber plane ?

A. Captain Robert Lewis   B. Captain Paul Tibbets
C. Iwo Jima   D. Enola Gay
E. Captain William Parsons

4. How many children were in the the family ?

A. 2   B. 6   C. 3
D. 4   E. 5

2.

5. Who prepared the bomb in the B-29 bomber ?

A. Captain Robert Lewis
B. Captain Paul Tibbets
C. Iwo Jima
D. Enola Gay
E. Captain William Parsons

6. What was the uniform of the women's college ?

A. white blouse, tartan hat, black skirt
B. red blouse, quilted hat, white skirt
C. white blouse, quilted hat, red skirt
D. white blouse, quilted hat, black skirt
E. black blouse, quilted hat, white skirt

7. Who was serving in the Japanese Imperial Army ?

A. Emiko's father
B. Emiko
C. Hideko
D. Tetsuro
E. Emiko's mother

8. How did the family soothe the sick child Aiko ?

A. By rubbing her head and holding her arms.
B. By rubbing her legs and holding her head.
C. By rubbing her arms and legs.
D. By rubbing her head and arms.
E. By rubbing her feet and legs.

9. Which of the following is **FALSE** ?

A. Emiko and Hideko caught the seven-o-clock train to Hiroshima.
B. Emiko and Tetsuro were brother and sister.
C. The pilot of the B-29 bomber was Captain Parsons.
D. Emiko's father was an antique dealer.
E. The name of the bomb was Little Boy.

10. Which of the following is **TRUE** ?

A. Emiko's mother was a cook.
B. The name of the aeroplane was Little Boy.
C. Emiko was thirteen years old.
D. The name of the B-29 bomber was Enola Gay.
E. The B-29 bomber was flying over the Atlantic Ocean.

The following passage contains a number of mistakes. You have to find the mistakes. On each line there is either _one_ mistake or _no_ mistake. Find the group of words in which there is a mistake and mark the letter for it on your answer sheet. If there is no mistake, mark N.

First, look for the _spelling_ mistakes.

As Emiko chatted to her classmate in the shade of a

11. | concrite wall | she looked into | the sky and | saw a single | |
    | A | B | C | D | N |

12. | B-29 bomber. | It was exacxtly | 8.10 am. | People waiting | |
    | A | B | C | D | N |

13. | for a street-car | saw it too | while Emiko | became scared. | |
    | A | B | C | D | N |

14. | There was a | tremendus | greenish-white | flash in the | |
    | A | B | C | D | N |

15. | sky. Emiko | afterwards | remembered vaguly | that there | |
    | A | B | C | D | N |

16. | was a roaring | or a rushing | sound as well, | but she was | |
    | A | B | C | D | N |

17. | not sure for | just at that | momant she lost | consciousness. | |
    | A | B | C | D | N |

18. | When Emiko | came to she | was lieing on her | face about | |
    | A | B | C | D | N |

19. | fourty feet | away from where | she had been | standing. She | |
    | A | B | C | D | N |

20. | was not aware | of any pane.Her | first thought | was "I'm alive!" | |
    | A | B | C | D | N |

Now look for _punctuation_ mistakes.

21. | She lifted Her | head slowly and | looked about | her as it | |
    | A | B | C | D | N |

22. | was growing | dark ? The air | was seething | with dust | |
    | A | B | C | D | N |

4.

23. | and smoke and | there was a | smell of burning. | emiko felt | |
|---|---|---|---|---|
| A | B | C | D | N |

24. | somethin'g trickle | into her eyes, | tasted it | in her mouth. | |
|---|---|---|---|---|
| A | B | C | D | N |

25. | Gingerly she | put her hand to | her head an | on looking | |
|---|---|---|---|---|
| A | B | C | D | N |

26. | at her hand. | saw with shock | that it was | covered in blood. | |
|---|---|---|---|---|
| A | B | C | D | N |

27. | With a hurt | child!s panic, | Emiko, streaming | with blood | |
|---|---|---|---|---|
| A | B | C | D | N |

28. | from gashes | in her scalp, | ran blindly in | search of Her | |
|---|---|---|---|---|
| A | B | C | D | N |

mother and father.

Read this passage and answer the questions which follow. If there are any words you don't understand you may find them in the Glossary at the end of the test.

MARY JANE IGNORED

1.   When Mary Jane turned the corner into Church Street that morning she leaned against a shop-front to rest herself. Her tiny head was bent over and her hair, which was so daudy and unclean, covered her face. Her small hands clasped each
5.   other for warmth across the faded front of her frock. Around the corner was Marley Cottages with their small frost-gleaming gardens and gates that squeaked and freezing to touch.
      She tried each gate in turn. Her feeble knock was well known to the people who lived in Marley Cottages. That
10. morning some of them said, "It's that Ward one again; don't open the door. She has been around twice in the last week; it's too much of a good thing."
      Those who did respond to her had been uncooperative. They poked cross and harassed faces around half-open doors. Tell her
15. mammy, they said, it's at school she should have her and not out worrying poor people the likes of them. They had the mouths of their own to feed and the bellies of their own to fill and God knows that took some doing.

20. The school was in Church Street and children with satchels were already walking past. Occasionally Mary Jane could see a few paper books peeping out from an open flap and beside them a child's lunch and a bottle of milk. In the classroom there was a blackboard which had scrawled and poor writing which was difficult to understand. As Mary Jane tried to work out the
25. answers staring faces sniggered when she gave silly answers.

A local priest used to come into the classroom and asked the children questions about the gospels and bible stories and gave out sweets when the children answered questions. Mary Jane was sitting on her own at the back of the room but
30. didn't answer any questions and therefore didn't get any sweets. The priest noticed this and when he was leaving he gave Mary Jane a handful of sweets. When the priest had left the teacher took the sweets off her as a punishment and gave them out to the other pupils as reward for neatness in their work.
35. While walking home she had her head down and an old lady thought she was crying and asked her was she alright. The street was crowded with workmen moving about and middle-aged women doing their shopping. Mary Jane told the old lady that she was only going home but her mother had asked her to
40. look for bread at the convent. The old lady told her that it might be too late as the nuns would be closing the convent and the bread they supplied to the poor was usually given out in the morning.

Mary Jane turned round and ran as quickly as she could
45. up the street to the convent but she was too late. There were a number of people there who told her that she would have to come back in the morning. So, she was glad to turn homewards. She was tired and her bare feet moved reluctantly on the ice-cold pavement. Her brother Tommy might have got some bread from
50. his customers as he went around selling his bundles of sticks.

Picking her way through the litter-strewn wasteland, she skipped and danced about, watching her shadow bobbing and growing with the uneven rippling of the ground, looking forward to her brother having some food. The light of the wintry
55. sun shone brightly on everything and the sky was clear blue and fluffed a little with white cloud.

29. How did Mary Jane rest herself in the first paragraph ?

A. She lay down in a garden.
B. She leaned against a garden gate.
C. She sat at the corner of the street.
D. She lay in a house on Marley Street.
E. She leaned against a shop-front.

30. What was well-known about Mary Jane to the people in Marley Cottages ?

A.   ...her small hands.   B.   ...her tiny head and hair.
C.   ...her feeble knock.   D.   ...her daudy, unclean hair.
E.   ...faded front of her dress.

31. Why would the people in Marley Cottages feel that Mary Jane shouldn't be worrying them ?

A.   ...she poked cross faces around half-doors.
B.   ...they had the mouths of their own to feed.
C.   ...her mammy had said she was at school.
D.   ...she could see a few paper books at school.
E.   ...their gates were freezing and squeaked.

32. What did Mary Jane see in the schoolbags of those children who were going to school ?

A.   satchels and books.   B.   a bottle of milk and lunch.
C.   a bible and sweets.   D.   an atlas and pencil-case.
E.   bread and milk.

33. What did Mary Jane's teacher do when the priest had left the classroom ?

A.   ...she read the children stories from the bible.
B.   ...she scolded the class for not answering well.
C.   ...she wrote a poem on the blackboard.
D.   ...she took the sweets off Mary Jane.
E.   ...she gave the children paper books.

34. Who tried to comfort Mary Jane on her way home from school ?

A.   the priest   B.   some workers   C.   the teacher
D.   an old lady   E.   her brother Tommy

35. What was bobbing and growing on the ground ?

A.   the sun   B.   the sky   C.   a shadow
D.   a cloud   E.   the rain

36. Why was there no bread at the convent in the evening ?

A. ...the nuns kept it for themselves.
B. ...the old lady had taken all the bread home.
C. ...Mary Jane's brother got the bread.
D. ...the bread was usually given out in the morning.
E. ...the middle-aged shoppers got the bread.

37. Mary Jane's brother Tommy got bread

A. ...from the nuns when he went to the convent.
B. ...from the customers he sold sticks to.
C. ...from the shoppers in the street.
D. ...from the workers moving along the street.
E. ...from the family's neighbours in Marley Cottages.

38. The passage's main emphasis is

A. ...the generosity of the nuns in the convent.
B. ...the nastiness of the schoolteacher.
C. ...the people who lived in Marley Cottages.
D. ...the kindness of the priest.
E. ...about a poor family and their search for food.

39. In most of the passage Mary Jane's emotion would have been
sadness and desolation.
In the last paragraph her main emotion would have been

A. despair   B. hope   C. anger
D. anxiety   E. sorrow

40. Why did the people in Marley Cottages say, in **lines 10 and 11**,
"It's that Ward one again; don't open the door." ?

A. ...they thought she was selling sticks.
B. ...they thought she was begging for food.
C. ...they thought she was going to school.
D. ...they thought she was looking for their children.
E. ...they thought the priest had sent her.

41.   Mary Jane was treated in a kind manner by

A.   ...her mother and brother Tommy.
B.   ...the neighbours and the workmen.
C.   ...Tommy's customers and the nun.
D.   ...the old lady and the priest.
E.   ...her teacher and fellow pupils.

42.   The phrase used in **line 13**, **"Those who did respond to her had been uncooperative"**, means

A.   ...the people would answer her because they didn't know her.
B.   ...the people's answers were hard to understand.
C.   ...the people who did answer had been unhelpful.
D.   ...the cottages were said not to be gleaming with frost.
E.   ...the people who came out were supportive.

Read this passage and answer the questions which follow. If there are any words you don't understand you may find them in the Glossary at the end of the test.

WILLIAM and the LITTLE GIRL

1.   He was still thinking of the little girl when he reached home after having been kept in to finish his sums.
          Before tea he again   stood upon his imaginary platform behind his glass of water and addressed a hall full of people who listened to
5.   him spellbound. The little girl was in the front row. Interrupters as large as mountains   rose to defy him. He wrestled with them and flung them out one after the other like ninepins. The whole room rose to applaud him. The little girl gazed at him in rapt admiration. He bowed to show his appreciation, took a long drink of water and
10.   proceeded with the lecture till the tea-bell rang. Again his elder brother greeted him disapprovingly as he entered the dining-room.
          "Good Lord! What on earth have you been doing upstairs ? You've brought a great lump of plaster down from the ceiling. Are you keeping an elephant up there, or what ?"
15.   William gave him a dark look as in imagination he ejected him again from his lecture, sending him flying through the door and half-way down the flight of stairs that was just outside the lecture-room. Having thus disposed of Robert, he turned to his mother, prepared to defend at great length the state of his hair, face,
20.   hands, suit and boots. But instead of attacking these points she said, "I've had an invitation to tea for you tomorrow, William."

9.

"Where?" asked William without much enthusiasm.

"Mrs. Lacey. She has a little niece staying with her."

William's heart jumped. He was sure that it was the little girl.

25. Without changing his severe expression he said, "I don't want to go to tea with a girl."

"Oh, she's got a little boy staying with her as well. He's convalescing after measles. He's the son of an old school friend. He's just about your age, I believe."

30. "So what," grunted William shortly. This was showing his annoyance at everything, the boy, the girl, the tea-party, measles and the world in general. Dreamily he stretched out for a bun and just as dreamily he took a huge bite. In reality he was alone with the little girl walking along a country lane. He was talking to her

35. about every subject from beginning to end in Henry's dictionary. She was listening to him intently.

However when he went to tea with her it was quite different. The boy was such a boy as William had ever imagined. He was tall, gangly and lazy. He spoke with a very refined accent and talked of

40. his travels in Italy, Switzerland and the South of France, of all the theatres he had visited and the latest dances. There was no doubt the little girl admired him as she listened to him in the same manner that she had listened to William.

In reality she ignored William completely after one haughty

45. glance that took in his shock of wiry hair, his unfavourable features and his stocky untidy figure. William wasn't used to being ignored and set about trying to get noticed. He realised that his greater size and age wouldn't themselves make him popular so he had to think of other ways to impress the little girl.

50. He tried to provide some information from his lecture on civilisation, stating that he had given lectures to large crowds of people. However no matter how he tried he could not get the attention of the little girl.

43. According to the first 20 lines of the passage which of the following statements is **TRUE** ?

A. The little girl was at home.
B. An elephant was upstairs.
C. William was kept in to finish his sums.
D. William's younger brother greeted him.
E. The little girl had to finish her sums.

44. Which statement from **line 37** to the end of the passage is **FALSE** ?

A. William couldn't get the attention of the little girl.
B. William had wiry hair.
C. The boy was tall and lazy.
D. The boy had travelled to Spain and Germany.
E. William was older than the little girl.

45. Which phrase in the second paragraph tells you that William wasn't giving a real lecture to a real crowd of people ?

A. ...stood upon his imaginary platform.
B. ...proceeded with the lecture.
C. ...interrupters rose to defy him.
D. ...who listened to him spellbound.
E. ...He bowed in appreciation.

46. Who scolded William when he came downstairs ?

A. His mother.   B. The little girl.
C. Robert.   D. The little boy.
E. Mrs. Lacey.

47. Who was getting better after the measles ?

A. Mrs. Lacey   B. William
C. Robert.   D. The little boy.
E. The little girl.

48. Why was William trying to get noticed in the second last paragraph ?

A. because he didn't like his unfavourable features.
B. because the little girl wouldn't leave him alone.
C. because he was bigger and older than anyone.
D. because he had created a good impression on the little girl.
E. because he wasn't used to being ignored.

11.

49. What did William imagine he was going to do to his brother ?

A.   ...send him flying through the door and down the stairs.
B.   ...defend him for the state of his hair face and hands.
C.   ...give him an invitation to tea.
D.   ...give him the lump of plaster that came off the ceiling.
E.   ...send him up to his room.

50.   What was it about the boy that the little girl admired ?

A.   ...he was related to Mrs. Lacey, the little girl's aunt.
B.   ...he spoke with a refined accent and talked about his travels.
C.   ...he was brilliant at sports and dancing.
D.   ...he was was convalescing from the measles.
E.   ...he had a shock of wiry hair and a stocky figure.

51.   What brought William's imaginary lecture to an end in the second paragraph ?

A.   ...his mother called him.
B.   ...he woke up from a dream.
C.   ...he wrestled with the interrupters.
D.   ...the whole room applauded him.
E.   ...the bell for tea rang.

52.   Which of the following **did not** annoy William in the **paragraph** beginning with **line 30** ?

A.   the girl   B.   the measles   C.   the boy
D.   the bun   E.   the world

53.   What was the final thing that William tried to do to get the attention of the little girl ?

A.   ...he told her how haughty she was.
B.   ...he told her about his travels in Switzerland.
C.   ...he told her he lectured to large crowds.
D.   ...he highlighted his superior size and age.
E.   ...he walked her along a country lane.

54. In **line 8** which words are Adjectives ?

A. rose, admiration
B. rapt, little
C. applaud, gazed
D. them, him, he
E. as, to, and

55. What **"part of speech"** is civilisation, lectures and crowds in **line 51** ?

A. verbs
B. adverbs
C. nouns
D. adjectives
E. pronouns

General Section

To answer these questions, you may have to think about the passages you have read. Look back at these if you need to. Look also at the Index and Glossary.

56. (a) Which section of this test contains the most **Proper nouns** ?

A. the HIROSHIMA passage.
B. the passage MARY JANE IGNORED.
C. the General Section.
D. the passage WILLIAM and the LITTLE GIRL.

(b). Which section of this test contains the most **direct speech** ?

A. the HIROSHIMA passage.
B. the passage MARY JANE IGNORED.
C. the General Section.
D. the passage WILLIAM and the LITTLE GIRL.

57. (a) Which of the following **"parts of speech"** are describing words ?

A. nouns and adjectives
B. verbs and adverbs
C. nouns and verbs
D. adjectives and adverbs

(b). Which of the following is the best description of **ADVERBS** ?

A. ...they describe adjectives and nouns.
B. ...they describe nouns and pronouns.
C. ...they describe verbs, adjectives and adverbs.
D. ...they describe only verbs.

13.

58. (a) Which of the following is the **best** description of a Thesauraus ?

A. ...a reference book for information on scientific words.
B   ...a reference book for finding meanings of words.
C. ...a reference book giving words that have similar meanings.
D. ...a reference book for information about homonymns.

(b). Which of the following is the best meaning for the phrase
      "programme of evacuation" as used in **line 4** of the passage,
      HIROSHIMA.

A. planned destruction of the population.
B. planned movement of the population.
C. planned housing of the population.
D. planned count of the population.

59. (a) Which of the following is closest to the meaning of "**haughty
          glance**" as used in **lines 44 and 45** in the passage, WILLIAM
          and the LITTLE GIRL ?

A. cheeky look   B. swift glimpse
C. arrogant look   D. nasty sighting

(b). Which word in the GLOSSARY means the same as
      "captivated and charmed" ?

A. conventional   B. harassed
C. reluctantly   D. spellbound

60. (a) Look back at the first paragraph of the passage, HIROSHIMA.
          What is meant by the phrase **"fleet of US bombers"** ?

A. ...very fast planes from United States of America.
B. ...fireworks for halloween.
C. ...group of bombing planes from United States of America.
D. ...brand name for hot sweets.

(b). What **"part of speech"** are the words, **Emicho, Italy** and **Marley
      Cottages** from the INDEX ?

A. nouns   B. proper nouns
C. pronouns   D. verbs

GLOSSARY

conventional	customary, as usual.
evacuees	people moved from a place of danger
ordnance expert	weapons and military supplies
T.N.T. blockbuster	really big dynamite bomb
cirrus cloud	high wispy cloud
harassed	annoy or trouble constantly
demolition	knock down or destroy a building
uncooperative	not willing to help
reluctantly	unwillingly
spellbound	entranced, fascinated
convalescing	recovering after an illness or operation
rapt admiration	complete and full approval
gangly	tall, lanky and awkward

INDEX

NEW TRANSFER TESTS

MULTIPLE-CHOICE

ENGLISH

Practice Test 5

Guidance for completing this Test.

1. Read the passages carefully.

2. Read the questions thoroughly.

3. Read the answers carefully.

4. Choose what you think is the correct answer carefully.

5. Underline or circle the answer, immediately after the question.

6. Transfer the LETTER **A,B,C,D,E** or **N** to the answer sheet.

7. Make sure to mark the answer box like [—] not [⁄].

8. Check carefully that you have transferred your correct answer.

9. This test lasts for **50 minutes.**

PUPIL'S NAME _____

TOTAL MARK (Out of 60)	

Multiple Choice

Read this passage and answer the questions which follow. If there are any words you don't understand you may find them in the Glossary at the end of the test.

NEW SCHOOL FOR JOHN

1.   As John walked warily into the playground he could feel many eyes staring at him, like hawks hunting their prey as the eyes followed him wherever he went. There were various groups of boys, some playing football, some throwing a ball and some just

5.   standing around. In one corner he spotted a group of girls skipping and their screaming was deafening. Then the skipping stopped and the attention was turned to a girl who had tripped, fallen over and cut her knee. Blood was trickling down the lower part of her left leg while tears were streaming down her cheeks as

10.   she felt the pain in her knee.

        The playground was bathed in sunshine and shadows flitted rapidly over the rough ground as the balls hit the surface between the groups of children. The sounds of the plastic hitting the tarmac echoed like the crack of a circus whip. As eyes watched

15.   no-one helped, no-one appeared to care, no-one came to his rescue. He felt new, strange, unwanted. The groups of pupils huddled even tighter.

        John felt an overwhelming urge to walk out of the gate through which he had entered not long before. Then as his heart

20.   quickened its pace, he found himself walking faster and faster before breaking into a run. He felt tears prickle his eyes. Everything in front of him seemed blurred and then John knew he was crying for real.

        He had reached the gate and fumbled with the latch as his

25.   fingers trembled in his anxiety. It wouldn't move. He couldn't open it. He was imprisoned. It was no use trying; he was locked in like a prisoner not allowed to escape. John kicked the gate in extreme torment. A persistent bell rang, reverberating inside his head like a metal ball in a game of pinball, every ring a score of

30.   fifty against his heart.

        The hairs on the back of John's neck spiked as if to warn danger. He froze, stationary by the gate, rigid with fear. The playground was slowly emptying as the children were steadily and relentlessly being sucked into the large three-storey grey

35.   building which stood tall like a fortress. It was like watching a monster enticing its victims. A new school day was beginning and John, still unable to move was spotted by the headmistress.

        She knew that a new boy was to commence school that day

40. but had thought that the boy's mother would have brought him into the school before school began. Miss Truman saw immediately the distress that John was in and realised that he was in a terrified state. She asked another teacher to take charge and headed towards the gate in a slow, deliberate but friendly manner, smiling all the time.

45. She spoke in a calm reassuring manner and gradually persuaded John to let go of the gate. Her quiet but effective words of comfort meant that John was content to follow her in to her office and by the time he had sat down and was drinking a glass of orange his fears had eased and Miss Truman had managed

50. to bring the smile to his face and proceeded to contact his mother to inform her of his distress.

Answer the following questions. Look back over the passage. You should choose the _best_ answer and mark its letter on your answer sheet.

1. Why do you think John was unable to open the gate in **lines 25 and 26** ?

A. ...he couldn't move because of his anxiety.
B. ...he was being chased by other pupils.
C. ...the teacher was shouting at him.
D. ...the school bell was ringing.
E. ...his father was outside the gate telling him not to leave.

2. In the last verse how did the headmistress persuade John to let go of the gate ?

A. ...she warned him that he was in serious trouble.
B. ...she told him that the other children would tease him.
C. ...she promised that she would give him sweets.
D. ...she spoke in a quiet, calm, comforting manner.
E. ...she said that she would bring him home.

3. What was the name of the headmistress ?

A. Miss Bowman   B. Miss Falseman   C. Miss Trueman
D. Miss Toughman   E. Miss Truman

4. In what type of mood did the headmistress move towards the gate where John was ?

A. ...angry and determined.   B. ...speedy and deliberate.
C. ...unhurried and friendly.   D. ...dominant and bossy.
E. ...distressed and hurried.

2.

5. As he first walked into the playground John was being watched by

A. hawks and other birds   B. teachers and parents
C. the eyes of the pupils   D. the caretaker
E. his mother and father

6. In what way did John move towards the school gate ?

A. with lengthy strides   B. with a quickening pace
C. in a slow, jovial manner   D. shouting and roaring
E. surrounded by school pals

7. How is the playground described as the balls fly around hitting the surface of the playground ?

A. dark and damp   B. full of brightness
C. echoes of screaming   D. windy and dull
E. happy and full of leaves

8. The little girl who fell had blood and tears on her

A. head and face   B. cheeks and knee
C. arms and ears   D. eyes and feet
E. legs and nose

9. Why was the playground becoming empty when John was at the school gate trying to leave ?

A. ...cars were being parked.
B. ...the teachers were arriving.
C. ...it started to rain.
D. ...the school day was ending.
E. ...the school bell was calling the pupils in.

10. The events in this passage happened

A. ...at the end of school.   B. ...at lunch-time.
C. ...at the beginning of school.   D. ...at break-time.
E. ...during the holidays.

The following passage contains a number of mistakes. You have to find the mistakes. On each line there is either _one_ mistake or _no_ mistake. Find the group of words in which there is a mistake and mark the letter for it on your answer sheet. If there is no mistake, mark N.

First, look for the _spelling_ mistakes.

11. Imagine, if you can, a small room, hezagonal in shape,
      A   B   C   D   N

12. like the cell of a bee. It is lighted neether by window
      A   B   C   D   N

13. nor by lamp, yet it is filed with a soft radiance. There
      A   B   C   D   N

14. are no apertures for ventilatation, yet the air was fresh
         A   B   C   D   N

15. and vibrant. Their are no musical instruments and
         A   B   C   D   N

16. yet at the same momant that my meditation begins,
         A   B   C   D   N

17. this space is throbbing with the most wonderfull melodic
         A   B   C   D   N

18. sounds. There, in the midst of such solace sits a small
         A   B   C   D   N

19. woman covered in fluffy garments but with a face as
         A   B   C   D   N

20. white as a sheet. This little room belunged to this lady.
         A   B   C   D   N

Now look for _punctuation_ mistakes.

21. A door bell rang. and the woman touched a switch.
         A   B   C   D   N

The music fell silent.
22. "I suppose i must see who that is," she thought as she set
         A   B   C   D   N

23. the chair in motion. the chair, like the music was worked
      A   B   C   D   N

24. by machinery and it rolled Her smoothly to the other side
      A   B   C   D   N

25. of the special room, where the bell rang persistently.
      A   B   C   D   N

26. "Who is it !" she called. Her voice was irritable, for she
      A   B   C   D   N

27. had been interrupted so many times since the music began ?
      A   B   C   D   N

28. When she listene'd into the receiver her white face broke
      A   B   C   D   N

into a smile as she recognised the voice of a dear friend.

**Read this passage and answer the questions which follow.
If there are any words you don't understand you may find
them in the Glossary at the end of the test.**

LEARNING TO DRIVE

1.   It is not an easy task for most people to learn to
drive a car. The thought of getting into a car for the first
time and being able to get it from one point to the next has
to be frightening. First of all you have to master the steering
5.   and become familiar with the steering wheel. Changing gear
is the next awkward procedure you have to undertake with
the first rule being able to avoid looking at the gear stick when
changing gear instead of concentratring on the road and
the traffic.
10.   In addition to looking at the traffic and road ahead
you must constantly check the traffic to your rear. There
is only one way to find out what the traffic behind is doing.
You must frequently check both the in-car mirror and the wing
mirrors. Indeed, driving instructors usually say to their
15. learners, "Look in the mirror first and then signal your
intention." This emphasises that mirrors aren't to be forgotten.

Once learner drivers have had a number of lessons their
instructor will be able to determine when they are in a position
to take the official Driving Test. The number of lessons required
20. for this will vary from learner to learner. Each applicant
has to undergo a theory and a practical test.
For the practical test the learner, who must be at least
seventeen years old, will be asked to drive through the streets
of a town near to where they live. The examiner will
25. accompany them, telling them what to do and what
procedures he wants the learner to perform. The examiner may say
to the learner, " Turn left at the next street and stop
opposite the Fire Station close to the footpath." He may then be
asked to carry out a three-point turn so that the car is turned and
30. facing in the direction from which it had come.
Other procedures may follow as the examiner tests the
learner driver on their driving skills, their awareness of traffic
and their ability to deal with motoring emergencies. One of
the areas with which most learners have difficulty when they are
35. undergoing a test is their nerves. It is perfectly natural to
experience nerves and most examiners will take account of
this as long as the learner doesn't make any errors which
might endanger the occupants of the test car or indeed
other road users.
40. Learning to drive properly is vital for the good of all
road users and passing the Driving Test is one of the highlights
of a person's young life. However it also places a serious
responsibility on the new driver as they join the vast group
of people who drive vehicles. The new drivers must realise
45. that they have a great responsibility to ensure they play their
part in making the roads and motorways of the country
safer places to drive.

29. What is the minimum age at which you are allowed to
drive on the public road ?

A. 18   B. 21   C. 17
D. 16   E. 20

30. According to the passage what is the first thing that the learner
has to master ?

A. ...the handbrake.   B. ...the rear-view mirror.
C. ...the gear stick.   D. ...the steering wheel.
E. ...the radio and CD player.

31. According to the passage what is the first thing the learner driver is told to do before actually driving ?

A. Check in the rear-view mirrors.
B. Put the car in gear.
C. Let off the handbrake.
D. Adjust the height of the seat.
E. Clean the steering wheel.

32. How many lessons does a learner driver take before doing the practical test ?

A. 10 lessons   B. 15 lessons   C. 20 lessons
D. ...as many as the instructor determines.
E. ...until the learner reaches 18 years of age.

33. According to the passage what is said to be one of the highlights of a young person's life ?

A. ...the first time they actually drive a car.
B. ...sitting the theory part of the driving test.
C. ...passing the practical section of the driving test.
D. ...going to do the driving test.
E. ...the thought of getting into a car for the first time.

34. What emotion best describes how a learner feels when getting into a car to learn to drive ?

A. ...elation   B. ...fear   C. sorrow
D. ...confidence   E. ...arrogance

35. In the second last paragraph the author highlights one of the difficulties from which most learner drivers suffer ? This is

A. ...keeping any passengers in the car safe.
B. ...awareness of other traffic and road users.
C. ...carrying out a three-point turn.
D. ...experiencing nerves.
E. ...their driving skills.

36. Which word in the first paragraph means the same as **"focussing"** ?

A. master   B. concentrating   C. changing
D. steering   E. frightening

SET 2 Blank Answer Sheets
ENGLISH Test 4
ENGLISH Test 5
ENGLISH Test 6

Instructions for completing the Answer Sheet.

1. You must concentrate fully when recording your answers.

   --take your time when recording your answers--

   --make sure you have the correct answer number--

   --make sure you select the correct letter, A, B, C, D, E or N--

2. Use a pencil to mark your answer, A, B, C, D, E or N.

3. Mark your answer like this---- (A̶) (B) (C) (D) (E) (N)

   (A) (B) (C̶) (D) (E) (N)

   (A) (B) (C) (D) (E) (N̶)

   ALWAYS USE A HORIZONTAL (—) LINE

4. DO NOT MARK like this-- (A) (B) (C) (D̸) (E) (N)

   (A) (B) (C̸) (D) (E) (N)

   (A) (B̸) (C) (D) (E) (N)

   (A) (B) (C) (D) (E̸) (N)

5. If you make a mistake, rub out the line, select the correct answer and draw a line through the correct letter.

6. It might be an idea to answer 5 questions at a time and then record these 5 answers all at the same time.

7. When reading the questions you record the answers on the question paper. When you have completed 5 questions on the question paper you then record these on the Answer sheet. Proceed to record another 5 questions.

ANSWER SHEETS — English Test 4

Please mark the boxes like (—), not like (╱). Rub out mistakes thoroughly.

Pages 2 & 3.

1 (A) (B) (C) (D) (E)	6 (A) (B) (C) (D) (E
2 (A) (B) (C) (D) (E)	7 (A) (B) (C) (D) (E)
3 (A) (B) (C) (D) (E)	8 (A) (B) (C) (D) (E)
4 (A) (B) (C) (D) (E)	9 (A) (B) (C) (D) (E)
5 (A) (B) (C) (D) (E)	10 (A) (B) (C) (D) (E)

Pages 4 — Spelling

11 (A) (B) (C) (D) (N)	16 (A) (B) (C) (D) (N)
12 (A) (B) (C) (D) (N)	17 (A) (B) (C) (D) (N)
13 (A) (B) (C) (D) (N)	18 (A) (B) (C) (D) (N)
14 (A) (B) (C) (D) (N)	19 (A) (B) (C) (D) (N)
15 (A) (B) (C) (D) (N)	20 (A) (B) (C) (D) (N)

Page 4 & 5 — Punctuation

21 (A) (B) (C) (D) (N)	25 (A) (B) (C) (D) (N)
22 (A) (B) (C) (D) (N)	26 (A) (B) (C) (D) (N)
23 (A) (B) (C) (D) (N)	27 (A) (B) (C) (D) (N)
24 (A) (B) (C) (D) (N)	28 (A) (B) (C) (D) (N)

Pages 6, 7, 8 & 9.

29 (A) (B) (C) (D) (E)	36 (A) (B) (C) (D) (E)
30 (A) (B) (C) (D) (E)	37 (A) (B) (C) (D) (E)
31 (A) (B) (C) (D) (E)	38 (A) (B) (C) (D) (E)
32 (A) (B) (C) (D) (E)	39 (A) (B) (C) (D) (E)
33 (A) (B) (C) (D) (E)	40 (A) (B) (C) (D) (E)
34 (A) (B) (C) (D) (E)	41 (A) (B) (C) (D) (E)
35 (A) (B) (C) (D) (E)	42 (A) (B) (C) (D) (E)

Pages 10, 11, 12 & 13.

43 (A) (B) (C) (D) (E)	49 (A) (B) (C) (D) (E)
44 (A) (B) (C) (D) (E)	50 (A) (B) (C) (D) (E)
45 (A) (B) (C) (D) (E)	51 (A) (B) (C) (D) (E)
46 (A) (B) (C) (D) (E)	52 (A) (B) (C) (D) (E)
47 (A) (B) (C) (D) (E)	53 (A) (B) (C) (D) (E)
48 (A) (B) (C) (D) (E)	54 (A) (B) (C) (D) (E)
	55 (A) (B) (C) (D) (E)

Pages 13 & 14 — General Section

56 (a) (A) (B) (C) (D)	58 (b) (A) (B) (C) (D)
(b) (A) (B) (C) (D)	59 (a) (A) (B) (C) (D)
57 (a) (A) (B) (C) (D)	(b) (A) (B) (C) (D)
(b) (A) (B) (C) (D)	60 (a) (A) (B) (C) (D)
58 (a) (A) (B) (C) (D)	(b) (A) (B) (C) (D)

Multiple Choice English
Test 4 Answer Key.

HIROSHIMA

1. B
2. E
3. A
4. D
5. E
6. D
7. D
8. C
9. C
10. D

Spelling

11. A--concrete
12. B--exactly
13. N
14. B--tremendous
15. C--vaguely
16. N
17. C--moment
18. C--lying
19. A--forty
20. B--pain

Punctuation

21. A--her
22. B--no question mark
23. D--Emiko
24. A--no apostrophe
25. N
26. A--no full stop
27. B--no exclamation
28. D--her

MARY JANE

29. E
30. C
31. B
32. B
33. D
34. D
35. C
36. D
37. B
38. E
39. B
40. B
41. D
42. C

WILLIAM and the LITTLE GIRL

43. C
44. D
45. A
46. C
47. D
48. E
49. A
50. B
51. E
52. D
53. C
54. B
55. C

General Section

	(a)		(b)	
56.	(a)	A	(b).	D
57.	(a)	D	(b).	C
58.	(a)	C	(b).	B
59.	(a)	C	(b).	D
60.	(a)	C	(b).	B

Multiple Choice English

Test 5 Answer Key.

NEW SCHOOL FOR JOHN

1. A
2. D
3. E
4. C
5. C
6. B
7. B.
8. B.
9. E.
10. C

Spelling

11. C--hexagonal
12. D--neither
13. B--filled
14. B--ventilation
15. B--there
16. B--moment
17. D--wonderful
18. N
19. N
20. C--belonged

Punctuation

21. B--no full stop
22. A--capital I
23. B--no full stop
24. C--her
25. N
26. A--exclamation mark
27. D--no question mark
28. B--no apostrophe

LEARNING TO DRIVE

29. C
30. D
31. A
32. D
33. C
34. B
35. D
36. B
37. C
38. D
39. B
40. C
41. E
42. D

THE GLOUCESTER TAYLOR

43. C
44. C
45. D
46. D
47. B
48. D
49. C
50. A
51. A
52. E
53. D
54. C
55. E

General Section

	(a)		(b).
56.	B		C
57.	D		A
58.	D		B
59.	D		C
60.	D		B

Multiple Choice English

Test 6 Answer Key.

NEW SCHOOL FOR JOHN

1.   E
2.   C
3.   C
4.   E
5.   B
6.   D
7.   A
8.   B
9.   B
10. D

Spelling

11. C--done
12. B--their
13. D--no
14. D--knew
15. N
16. C--advice
17. B--brochures
18. D--some
19. A--bushes
20. N

Punctuation

21. B--were
22. D--no question mark
23. B--no full stop
24. A--Trench
25. N
26. B--no comma
27. B--old
28. B--no speech marks

MARY JANE IGNORED

29. D
30. B
31. E
32. B
33. E
34. A
35. E
36. C
37. C
38. C
39. B
40. A
41. D
42. D

CURIOUS EXPLORERS

43. C
44. B
45. E
46. A
47. D
48. E
49. C
50. D
51. B
52. D
53. B
54. D
55. C

General Section

	(a)		(b).	
56.	(a)	A	(b).	C
57.	(a)	D	(b).	B
58.	(a)	A	(b).	B
59.	(a)	D	(b).	C
60.	(a)	C	(b).	B

English Test 5

Please mark the boxes like (—), not like (╱). Rub out mistakes thoroughly.

Pages 2 & 3.

1	(A)(B)(C)(D)(E)	6	(A)(B)(C)(D)(E
2	(A)(B)(C)(D)(E)	7	(A)(B)(C)(D)(E)
3	(A)(B)(C)(D)(E)	8	(A)(B)(C)(D)(E)
4	(A)(B)(C)(D)(E)	9	(A)(B)(C)(D)(E)
5	(A)(B)(C)(D)(E)	10	(A)(B)(C)(D)(E)

Pages 4

Spelling

11	(A)(B)(C)(D)(N)	16	(A)(B)(C)(D)(N)
12	(A)(B)(C)(D)(N)	17	(A)(B)(C)(D)(N)
13	(A)(B)(C)(D)(N)	18	(A)(B)(C)(D)(N)
14	(A)(B)(C)(D)(N)	19	(A)(B)(C)(D)(N)
15	(A)(B)(C)(D)(N)	20	(A)(B)(C)(D)(N)

Page 4 & 5

Punctuation

21	(A)(B)(C)(D)(N)	25	(A)(B)(C)(D)(N)
22	(A)(B)(C)(D)(N)	26	(A)(B)(C)(D)(N)
23	(A)(B)(C)(D)(N)	27	(A)(B)(C)(D)(N)
24	(A)(B)(C)(D)(N)	28	(A)(B)(C)(D)(N)

Pages 6, 7, 8 & 9.

29	(A)(B)(C)(D)(E)	36	(A)(B)(C)(D)(E)
30	(A)(B)(C)(D)(E)	37	(A)(B)(C)(D)(E)
31	(A)(B)(C)(D)(E)	38	(A)(B)(C)(D)(E)
32	(A)(B)(C)(D)(E)	39	(A)(B)(C)(D)(E)
33	(A)(B)(C)(D)(E)	40	(A)(B)(C)(D)(E)
34	(A)(B)(C)(D)(E)	41	(A)(B)(C)(D)(E)
35	(A)(B)(C)(D)(E)	42	(A)(B)(C)(D)(E)

Pages 10, 11 & 12.

43	(A)(B)(C)(D)(E)	49	(A)(B)(C)(D)(E)
44	(A)(B)(C)(D)(E)	50	(A)(B)(C)(D)(E)
45	(A)(B)(C)(D)(E)	51	(A)(B)(C)(D)(E)
46	(A)(B)(C)(D)(E)	52	(A)(B)(C)(D)(E)
47	(A)(B)(C)(D)(E)	53	(A)(B)(C)(D)(E)
48	(A)(B)(C)(D)(E)	54	(A)(B)(C)(D)(E)
		55	(A)(B)(C)(D)(E)

Pages 13 & 14

General Section

56	a) (A)(B)(C)(D)	58	(b) (A)(B)(C)(D)
	b) (A)(B)(C)(D)	59	(a) (A)(B)(C)(D)
57	a) (A)(B)(C)(D)		(b) (A)(B)(C)(D)
	b) (A)(B)(C)(D)	60	(a) (A)(B)(C)(D)
58	a) (A)(B)(C)(D)		(b) (A)(B)(C)(D)

English Test 6

Please mark the boxes like (—), not like (╱). Rub out mistakes thoroughly.

Pages 2, 3 & 4.

1	(A) (B) (C) (D) (E)	6	(A) (B) (C) (D) (E)
2	(A) (B) (C) (D) (E)	7	(A) (B) (C) (D) (E)
3	(A) (B) (C) (D) (E)	8	(A) (B) (C) (D) (E)
4	(A) (B) (C) (D) (E)	9	(A) (B) (C) (D) (E)
5	(A) (B) (C) (D) (E)	10	(A) (B) (C) (D) (E)

Pages 4

Spelling

11	(A) (B) (C) (D) (N)	16	(A) (B) (C) (D) (N)
12	(A) (B) (C) (D) (N)	17	(A) (B) (C) (D) (N)
13	(A) (B) (C) (D) (N)	18	(A) (B) (C) (D) (N)
14	(A) (B) (C) (D) (N)	19	(A) (B) (C) (D) (N)
15	(A) (B) (C) (D) (N)	20	(A) (B) (C) (D) (N)

Page 5

Punctuation

21	(A) (B) (C) (D) (N)	25	(A) (B) (C) (D) (N)
22	(A) (B) (C) (D) (N)	26	(A) (B) (C) (D) (N)
23	(A) (B) (C) (D) (N)	27	(A) (B) (C) (D) (N)
24	(A) (B) (C) (D) (N)	28	(A) (B) (C) (D) (N)

Pages 6, 7, 8 & 9.

29	(A) (B) (C) (D) (E)	36	(A) (B) (C) (D) (E)
30	(A) (B) (C) (D) (E)	37	(A) (B) (C) (D) (E)
31	(A) (B) (C) (D) (E)	38	(A) (B) (C) (D) (E)
32	(A) (B) (C) (D) (E)	39	(A) (B) (C) (D) (E)
33	(A) (B) (C) (D) (E)	40	(A) (B) (C) (D) (E)
34	(A) (B) (C) (D) (E)	41	(A) (B) (C) (D) (E)
35	(A) (B) (C) (D) (E)	42	(A) (B) (C) (D) (E)

Pages 10, 11 & 12.

43	(A) (B) (C) (D) (E)	49	(A) (B) (C) (D) (E)
44	(A) (B) (C) (D) (E)	50	(A) (B) (C) (D) (E)
45	(A) (B) (C) (D) (E)	51	(A) (B) (C) (D) (E)
46	(A) (B) (C) (D) (E)	52	(A) (B) (C) (D) (E)
47	(A) (B) (C) (D) (E)	53	(A) (B) (C) (D) (E)
48	(A) (B) (C) (D) (E)	54	(A) (B) (C) (D) (E)
		55	(A) (B) (C) (D) (E)

Pages 12, 13 & 14

General Section

56	(a) (A) (B) (C) (D)	58	(b) (A) (B) (C) (D)
	(b) (A) (B) (C) (D)	59	(a) (A) (B) (C) (D)
57	(a) (A) (B) (C) (D)		(b) (A) (B) (C) (D)
	(b) (A) (B) (C) (D)	60	(a) (A) (B) (C) (D)
58	(a) (A) (B) (C) (D)		(b) (A) (B) (C) (D)

37.　In the Practical part of the Driving test the learner

A.　...answers written questions on a test paper.
B.　...drives through the streets on his/her own.
C.　...drives through the streets with his/her examiner.
D.　...drives through the streets with his/her instructor.
E.　...answers questions from his/her instructor.

38.　What happens when a car makes a **three-point turn** ?

A.　...it touches the kerbs in three places.
B.　...it turns in the road four times.
C.　...it starts three times after the key is turned.
D.　...it turns so that it faces in the opposite direction.
E.　...the driver has to turn the car in a three-metre space.

39.　To undergo the Practical Driving test applicants have to

A.　...go to Belfast to a specialised test centre.
B.　...go to a town near them to take the test through the streets.
C.　...sit in a stationary vehicle and carry out driving skills.
D.　...take the test along the street or the road where they live.
E.　...sit at a computer and carry out tasks which simulate real driving.

40.　The main emphasis of the passage is

A.　...highlighting how easy it is to pass the Driving test.
B.　...to provide learners drivers with all the skills they need.
C.　...to give general information on learning to drive and the test.
D.　...to show how understanding Test Examiners are.
E.　...to encourage young people to learn to drive and buy a car.

41.　The phrase, **"to deal with motoring emergencies"** is used in **line 33** of the passage. It means

A.　to call the ambulance and paramedics.
B.　to remove crashed vehicles from an accident scene.
C.　to administer first aid at the scene of a car crash.
D.　to carry out car repairs when a car breaks down.
E.　to be aware of other traffic and take necessary driving action.

42. The TWO verbs in **Line 26** are

A. what / learner
B. examiner / perform
C. procedures / what
D. perform / wants
E. learner / examiner

Read this passage and answer the questions which follow. If there are any words you don't understand you may find them in the Glossary at the end of the test.

THE GLOUCESTER TAILOR

1.   In the time of swords and periwigs and full-skirted coats with flowered lappets when gentlemen wore ruffles, and gold-laced waistcoats of quilted silk and taffeta there lived a tailor in Gloucester. He sat in the window of a little shop in Westgate Street,

5.   cross-legged on a table, from morning till dark.
      All day long while the light lasted he sewed and snippeted, piecing out his satin and cashmere, and lutestring; cloths had strange names, and were very expensive in the days of the Tailor of Gloucester. But although he sewed fine silk for his

10. neighbours, he himself was very, very poor, a little old man in spectacles, with a pinched face, old crooked fingers, and a suit of thread-bare clothes, since he was paid very little.
      He cut his coats without waste, according to his embroidered cloth; they were very small ends and snippets that lay about upon

15. the table. "Too narrow breadths for nothing except waistcoats for mice," said the tailor.
      One bitter, cold day near Christmas-time the tailor began to make a coat of cherry-coloured corded silk embroidered with pansies and roses, and a cream coloured satin waistcoat trimmed

20. with gauze and green-worsted chenille for the Mayor of Gloucester.
      The tailor worked and worked, and he talked to himself. He measured the silk, and turned it round and round, and trimmed it into shape with his shears; the table was all littered

25. with cherry-coloured snippets. "No breadth at all, and cut on the cross; it is no breadth at all; tippets for mice and ribbons for mobs for mice!" said the Tailor of Gloucester.
      When the snow-flakes came down against the small leaded window-panes and shut out the light, the tailor had done his day's

30. work; all the silk and satin lay cut out upon the table.

There were twelve pieces for the coat and four pieces for the waistcoat; and there were pocket flaps and cuffs, and buttons all in order. For the lining of the coat there was fine yellow taffeta; and for the button-holes of the waistcoat, there was
35. cherry-coloured twist. And everything was ready to sew together in the morning, all measured and sufficient except that there was wanting just one single skein of cherry-coloured twisted silk.

The tailor came out of his shop at dark, for he did not sleep there at nights; he fastened the window and locked the door, and
40. took away the key. No one lived there at night but little brown mice, and they run in and out without any keys !

For behind the wooden wainscots of all the old houses in Gloucester, there are little mouse staircases and secret trap-doors; and the mice run from house to house through those long narrow
45 passages; they can run all over the town without going into the streets. But the tailor came out of his shop, and shuffled home through the snow. He lived quite near by in College Court, next to the doorway to College Green; and although it was not a big house, the tailor was so poor he only rented the kitchen.
50 He lived alone with his cat; it was called Simpkin. Now all day long while the tailor was out at work, Simpkin kept house by himself; and he also was fond of the mice, though he gave them no satin for coats !

43. For how long did the tailor work each day ?

A. From morning till morning.
B. From six in the morning till six at night.
C. From morning till dark.
D. From night till morning.
E. From eight in the morning till eight at night.

44. The coat made for the Mayor of Gloucester was made from

A. embroidered cloth   B. pompadour and lutestring
C. embroidered corded silk   D. roses and pansies
E. gauge and chenille

45. Where did the tailor do his work ?

A. in the attic   B. in a workshop
C. in his house   D. in a shop window
E. in his kitchen

46. Why were the mice able to run all over the town without going into the streets ?

A.   ...they run through the sewers under the houses.
B.   ...they have keys to all the doors of the houses.
C.   ...they run across the attics of the houses.
D.   ...they have little mouse stairs and secret trap-doors.
E.   ...there were no cats in this town to stop them.

47. At what time of the year was the tailor making the Mayor's coat ?

A.   Summer   B.   Christmas
C.   Halloween   D.   Easter
E.   Autumn

48. Which THREE tasks did the tailor carry out when he left his shop at night ?

A.   ..switched lights, closed doors and left the key under the mat.
B.   ..locked windows, opened doors and hid the key.
C.   ..tidied tools, stored materials and took the key.
D.   ..took the key, locked the door and closed the windows.
E.   ..cut the satin, tidied the buttons and locked all the cupboards.

49. Why do you think the old tailor was very, very, poor ?

A.   ...he made expensive clothes.
B.   ...the mice destroyed all his material.
C.   ...his customers didn't pay him enough.
D.   ...he worked very few hours.
E.   ...he didn't work long enough.

50. How was the tailor able to see to make the clothes ?

A.   Using the daylight.
B.   Using electric light.
C.   Using light from an oil lamp.
D.   Using light from candles.
E.   Using the light from the street lamps.

11.

51. What did the tailor use for the waistcoat's button holes ?

A.   ...cherry-coloured twist.   B.   ...fine yellow taffeta.
C.   ...cherry-coloured silk.   D.   ...cream-coloured silk.
E.   ...green-worsted chenille.

52. How many pieces of cloth had been laid out on the table when the tailor went home on the bitter-cold day near Christmas ?

A.   2 pieces
B.   4 pieces
C.   8 pieces
D.   12 pieces
E.   16 pieces

53. Which of the following is the best description of the tailor ?

A.   ...strong, tall, jolly and well-dressed.
B.   ...young, small, frail and prosperous.
C.   ...small, old, rich and wore glasses.
D.   ...old, very poor, crooked fingers and small.
E.   ...poorly dressed, healthy face, tall and wore spectacles.

54. What does the phrase **"and shuffled home"** tell us about the tailor ?

A.   ...he couldn't get a bus home.
B.   ...there was a lot of snow.
C.   ...he was old, frail and tired.
D.   ...he was in a hurry to get home.
E.   ...he didn't want to slip and fall over.

55. **Line 11** reads, **'spectacles, with a pinched face, old crooked fingers, and a'** .
Which pair of words below are nouns ?

A.   spectacles / with
B.   pinched / face
C.   fingers / crooked
D.   old /and
E.   spectacles / face

12.

General Section

To answer these questions, you may have to think about the passages you have read. Look back at these if you need to. Look also at the Index and Glossary.

56. (a) In which kind of a publication would you find writing which doesn't have proper sentences ?

A. a novel   B. a diary
C. a magazine   D. an essay

(b). In which kind of a publication would you find writing which is completely non-fictional ?

A. a novel
B. a comic
C. an encyclopedia
D. a poem

57. (a) Which of the following is the best description of a pronoun ?

A. a word which describes how something is done.
B. a word used to join words or phrases or parts of sentences.
C. a word which expresses sudden emotion.
D. a word which takes the place of a noun.

(b). Which pair of the following are correct plurals ?

A. oxen and salmon
B. son-in-laws and sheep
C. monkies and thiefs
D. childs and hoofes

58. (a) Which of the following have no singular form ?

A. echoes
B. loaves
C. feet
D. scissors

In each of the following questions you have to choose the *best word* or *group of words* to complete this passage so that it makes sense.
Choose one of the answers and mark the letter on the answer sheet.

It was the day that the Inspector came to our wee school. We had

58. (b).   been   telled   told   entold   tolled   that there would be a
                      A   B   C   D

59. (a) meeting between the   principle   principla   princpel   principal
                                    A   B   C   D

(b).   and   the   three   teachers   whose   whom   who   that
                                          A   B   C   D

60. (a) taut   teached   learned   taught   in the school. The pupils were
          A   B   C   D

(b).   asked to   rite   write   right   wright   a story during this meeting.
                    A   B   C   D

14.

GLOSSARY

persistent----- continuous or constant
reverberating- echoing or vibrating
fortress-------- castle, fort or stronghold
enticing------- coaxing, luring, persuading
meditation---- reflection, pondering, studying
melodic-------- tuneful, musical
procedure----- method, practice, strategy
emphasises--- stresses, give priority, highlights
emergency---- crisis, difficulty, predicament
periwig-------- type of wig
lappets-------- decorative flap on headgear
taffeta--------- crisp smooth woven fabric usually made from silk
cashmere----- type of woolen fabric
lutestring----- type of silk from a moth
chenille------- special yarn usually made from cotton
embroidered-- decorated with needlework
skein---------- a long coil of yarn or hair
wainscot------ wooden cladding on inside walls of a room

INDEX

15.

NEW TRANSFER TESTS

MULTIPLE-CHOICE

ENGLISH

Practice Test 6

Guidance for completing this Test.

1. Read the passages carefully.

2. Read the questions thoroughly.

3. Read the answers carefully.

4. Choose what you think is the correct answer carefully.

5. Underline or circle the answer, immediately after the question.

6. Transfer the LETTER **A,B,C,D,E** or **N** to the answer sheet.

7. Make sure to mark the answer box like [—] not [/].

8. Check carefully that you have transferred your correct answer.

9 . This test lasts for **50 minutes.**

PUPIL'S NAME _____

TOTAL MARK (Out of 60)	

Read this passage and answer the questions which follow. If there are any words you don't understand you may find them in the Glossary at the end of the test.

THE VEGETABLE PLOT

1.   How a country is dealing with its economic and social needs can be gauged by the level of involvement by its citizens in vegetable growing. It is a fact that, in times when jobs are scarce and people are finding the economic side of living

5.   hazardous, an increasing number of people decide to try and provide for themselves.
       Those who see the need to do something for themselves usually turn to the vegetable plot to ease the burden of the weekly food bill. As a result of the recent downturn in the

10.   economy, the Trench family decided to use part of their rear garden to grow vegetables. Preparation was important.
All members of the Trench family would be involved.
       Daddy Trench was to be assisted by his seventeen year old son, Frank and thirteen year old Annie was also

15.   to assist. Mindful of the fact that the garden had never been used for vegetables for a long time, they decided to begin in the winter to prepare the ground. Daddy and Frank decided on a large plot and Annie drew white lines around the part that was to be dug.

20.   Father and son got stuck into digging the plot. They soon realised that it was going to be a mammoth job, especially since neither of them had ever done any manual work. Parts of their bodies that they hardly knew existed before were now on fire with the aches and pains that come from using muscles that are

25.   rarely used.
       Machinery was needed and so to the local Hire Shop where they hired out a rotavator, a machine which helped to achieve the result they wanted, a large plot of well dug and raked soil that looked so healthy, clean and free

30.   from weeds.
       They were advised to contact a local farmer and obtain a load of farmyard manure, which they got for a meagre amount of money. They spread the manure all over the cultivated soil leaving it to penetrate the soil, adding much needed nutrients.

35.   Spring came and Daddy, Frank and Annie were now joined by Mammy Trench who got involved in choosing the plants and seeds that were to be used to provide the household vegetables for

40. the following Summer and Autumn. They decided that in the vegetable plot they would grow peas, beans, potatoes, cabbages, cauliflowers, beetroot, carrots, parsnips, lettuce, leeks, scallions and celery.

It was also decided to grow tomatoes and strawberries in hanging baskets to be hung from the new gazebo that Daddy had constructed the previous year. The planting took place over a period
45. of three days with Daddy and Annie being responsible for this.

Pride and a real sense of achievement were felt by the family who were now prepared to wait both in expectation and trepidation to see the fruits of their labours. It remains to be seen if the Trench family have "green fingers".

Answer the following questions. Look back over the passage. You should choose the _best_ answer and mark its letter on your answer sheet.

1. Why had the Trench family decided to grow vegetables ?

A. They wanted to utilise their large garden.
B. Annie had an interest in gardening.
C. They were encouraged by the government.
D. The family needed fresh vegetables.
E. Because of the downturn in the economy.

2. When do people decide to try and provide for themselves ?

A. When the whole family all have jobs.
B. When the price of vegetables increases.
C. When there are few jobs and finances are hazardous.
D. When renovations have been carried out to the house.
E. When the Government raises taxes.

3. How long did it take to plant out the vegetable plot ?

A. a day   B. two days   C. three days
D. a week   E. a month

4. How many types of vegetables did the Trench family plant in the vegetable plot ?

A. four   B. six   C. eight
D. ten   E. twelve

2.

5.   What advantage does a family who grow their own vegetables
     gain as a result of having their own vegetables ?

A.   Showing up their neighbours.
B.   They reduce the cost of their weekly food bill.
C.   Being able to sell them for added finance.
D.   They didn't have as much grass to cut.
E.   They didn't watch as much TV as before.

6.   The main reason that Daddy and son Frank found the
     job of digging a huge job was

A.   ...they didn't have enough money to buy the materials.
B.   ...they couldn't operate the machinery they hired.
C.   ...the plot was a little too small.
D.   ...they hadn't ever done any physical work.
E.   ...they had to listen to all the suggestions of Mammy and Annie.

7.   How did the farmyard manure help grow good vegetables ?

A.   ...it went into the soil, adding nutrients to them.
B.   ...it added flavour and a scent to them.
C.   ...it prevented the weeds from choking them.
D.   ...it broke up the soil, adding moisture to them.
E.   ...it was needed to provide warmth for them.

8.   The two main contributions of Mammy Trench and Annie were

A.   ...digging the ground and planting.
B.   ...choosing plants and marking out the plot.
C.   ...digging the ground and choosing plants.
D.   ...choosing plants and spreading manure.
E.   ...spreading manure and marking the plot.

9.   In what condition did the rotavator leave the ground ?

A.   full of lumps and uneven   B.   clean, healthy, weedless
C.   fine, sandy, uneven soil   D.   weedy, even, healthy
E.   unchanged from before its use

3.

10. What is meant by the last phrase of the passage ,
    " the Trench family have 'green fingers ' " ?

A. they had painted the garden fence green.
B. they had handled the vegetables without gloves.
C. they had got rid of the pest, the greenfly.
D. they had the gift of successfully growing plants.
E. they only grew green vegetables.

The following passage contains a number of mistakes. You have to find the mistakes. On each line there is either _one_ mistake or _no_ mistake. Find the group of words in which there is a mistake and mark the letter for it on your answer sheet. If there is no mistake, mark N.

First, look for the _spelling_ mistakes.

11. Once all the | planting had | been don in | the Spring the
        A   B   C   D   N

12. Trench family | admired there | work but | realised that
        A   B   C   D   N

13. a number of | other tasks were | ahead of them. | Having know
        A   B   C   D   N

14. previous experience | of vegetable | growing they | new that
        A   B   C   D   N

15. they had | to consult. | They visited a | number of Garden
        A   B   C   D   N

16. Centres, | always seeking | advise and | guidance and
        A   B   C   D   N

17. collecting | broshures about | planting and | growing. In
        A   B   C   D   N

18. addition they | were picking up | extra plants | and sum
        A   B   C   D   N

19. fruit bushs | and trees. The | advice that they | were given
        A   B   C   D   N

20. ensured that | they had a list | of things to | design and make.
        A   B   C   D   N

4.

Now look for _punctuation_ mistakes.

21. One of the extra | jobs they we're | advised about | was protection   N
           A   B   C   D

22. of the plot from | predators such | as small | four? legged   N
            A   B   C   D

23. animals and birds. in their attempts at being economical   N
        A   B   C   D

24. Daddy trench | decided to erect | a fence using | old timber,   N
        A   B   C   D

25. posts and net | bags that had been | used to hold | firewood. These   N
        A   B   C   D

26. were attached to | the posts to, form | the fence and | then the whole   N
        A   B   C   D

27. plot was covered | with the Old | football nets | of the goalposts   N
        A   B   C   D

28. which were now | redundant." Since | the net bags | were different   N
        A   B   C   D

colours the nets, the posts and the whole plot looked well.

**Read this passage and answer the questions which follow.
If there are any words you don't understand you may find
them in the Glossary at the end of the test.**

MARY JANE IGNORED

1.   The MS Orion, a small white ship, was docked at Savannah,
Georgia. Simon Renier, hands in the pockets of his old-fashioned
grey trousers, looked at the vessel with mounting excitement.
He would be spending the next week on the Orion travelling to
5.   Venezuela and already standing on the pier in Savannah,
he was farther away from home than he had ever been in
all his thirteen years.
        It was a chilly February day, with a thin rain and a biting
wind. In a more sheltered part of the harbour stood his cousin,
10.   Forsyth Phair, with whom he would be travelling and his
great-aunt Leonis Phair, with whom he lived and who had
come with them on the train from Charleston to see them
off from the harbour.

As Simon looked at the two of them under their umbrellas
15. he couldn't help thinking that if he were travelling with Aunt
Leonis instead of cousin Forsyth he would be perfectly happy.
Aunt Leonis was comfort and all-rightness in a precarious world.
He had known cousin Forsyth for barely a month and while the
distinguished-looking middle-aged man was pleasant and
20. courteous he was not outgoing and still a stranger to Simon.
He looked damp and uncomfortable with the rain dripping
off his large black umbrella and the collar to his dark raincoat
turned up. Even the corners of his waxed moustache seemed to
droop. The old woman, on the other hand, stood straight as an
25. arrow, unperturbed by the downpour.
"Can't you come, too ?" Simon begged her.
"I'm too tired, child," the old woman had said. "At ninety
I've earned the right to my rocking chair and my books.
Besides I have to stay home and take care of Boz." The old dog in
30. pointer years was almost as old as Aunt Leonis. His proud
skeleton showed under the still-glossy liver-spotted body and
Simon felt a tightening of his stomach muscles as he realised
that he might not be there when he returned.
He turned his face into the rain and moved farther away
35. from Aunt Leonis and cousin Forsyth, past the gangplank of the
Orion and on down the dock. All around him was activity, the
tall yellow arms of the Orion swinging sacks of seeds and grain
and rice up onto the ship to be stored in the hold. Simon
watched in fascination as a large station wagon was carefully
40. hoisted from the dock, swung loose for a moment high in the
air then was lowered gently onto the foredeck.
On the aft deck stood the passengers, who had already
embarked at Brooklyn and Baltimore, eagerly watching the
business of loading the freighter. A few of them waved at him
45. and he waved shyly back.

29. At which two ports had the MS Orion called before arriving
in Savannagh ?

A.	Georgia and Savannah
B.	Venezuela and Charleston
C.	Orion and Charleston
D.	Brooklyn and Baltimore
E.	Savannah and Baltimore

30. The word **dock** is used in **line 36.** The **TWO** other words in the first two paragraphs that mean the same as **dock** are

A. vessel / part
C. train / harbour
E. pier / train

B. pier / harbour
D. harbour / ship

31. **Line 6** states that Simon Renier was farther away from home than he had ever been in his life. Where was this ?

A. ...in Venezuela.
C. ...on the MS Orion.
E. ...on the pier in Savannah.

B. ...in Charleston.
D. ...in Brooklyn.

32. For how long had Simon known his cousin Forsyth ?

A. ...all his life.
C. ...less than a year.
E. ...for thirteen years.

B. ...less than a month.
D. ...less than a week.

33. As Simon watched the MS Orion being loaded he was fascinated by

A. ...the ship's funnels.
B. ...the waving passengers.
C. ...the sacks of seeds and grain being loaded.
D. ...the sight of his cousin and aunt.
E. ...a large station wagon being loaded onto the ship.

34. The sacks of grain, rice and seeds were to be stored

A. ...in the hold.
C. ...in the cabins.
E. ...on the foredeck.

B. ...on the aft deck.
D. ...on the lower deck.

35. What reason did Simon's aunt offer when Simon asked her to join them on the trip ?

A. ...she was too old.
C. ...she had other travel plans.
E. ...she needed to read in her rocking chair.

B. ...she was too busy.
D. ...she hadn't an umbrella.

36. **Line 17** states that **"Aunt Leonis was comfort and all-rightness in a precarious world."** This means

A. ...she was too old to live in such a dangerous world.
B. ...she had lived in comfort and safety in a small country.
C. ...she was support, cool and OK in an unsafe world.
D. ...she was the life and soul of the party but uncharitable.
E. ...she was cranky, stubborn and selfish.

37. Which of the characters in the story are described as **polite**, **pleasant** and **distinguished** ?

A. great-aunt Leonis Phair.   B. Simon Renier.
C. cousin Forsyth Phair.   D. the passenger on the deck
E. the old woman.

38. Why were great-aunt Leonis and cousin Forsyth standing in a sheltered place ?

A. ...they were waiting to get off the ship.
B. ...they were protecting their luggage.
C. ...it was a chilly, rainy day with a cold wind.
D. ...there was no room on the pier for all the passengers.
E. ...it was warmer to stay in the shelter.

39. The words **still-glossy** and **liver-spotted** are

A. compound nouns.   B. hyphenated adjectives.
C. hyphenated verbs.   D. compound adjectives.
E. compound verbs.

40. The words **chilly**, **thin** and **biting** in **line 8** are

A. adjectives   B. pronouns
C. nouns   D. verbs
E. adverbs

41. The word closest in meaning to **precarious (line 17)** is

A. safe   B. cautious   C. happy
D. dangerous   E. changing

8.

42. What is meant by the phrase, **"tightening of his stomach muscles"** in **line 32** ?

A. ..becoming ill.
B. ..bracing his stomach.
C. ..feeling free and easy.
D. ..feeling anxious and worried.
E. ..strengthening his stomach.

Read this passage and answer the questions which follow. If there are any words you don't understand you may find them in the Glossary at the end of the test.

CURIOUS EXPLORERS

1.   Men have always been curious about the world in which they live. Since the beginning of civilisation people have had the instinct to go and find out about the world. Early man, such as those that were classed as cavemen had to explore in order to
5. survive. Their main focus would have been to provide shelter and find food for themselves and their families.

      Once these basics were looked after they probably felt the need to find out more about their environment. They must have wondered how far the forest that surrounded them stretched.
10. Where did the river, which provided them with water, begin and end ? What happened to the sun when the day ended ? What other animals were there besides those which they hunted for food and clothing ?

      These were questions that surely led to our earliest citizens
15. travelling beyond their own territory to discover new truths. It is known that in 2007 B.C. an Egyptian made an amazing journey by boat to the coast of Somaliland. The Minoan tribe from Crete explored the whole of the Mediterranean Sea in their small fishing boats around the same time.
20.   By 600 BC the Phoenicians, people originally from present day Lebanon, had ventured out of the Mediterranean and into the huge expanse of ocean, the Atlantic. They moved up the West coast of Europe and set the pattern for loads of other explorers such as the Greeks, the Romans and the Carthaginians. These
25. groups explored and investigated the Ancient regions of the Western world while the Chinese were the early explorers in the Far East of the world.

      The leaders of modern exploration were actually the Vikings who were probably the first group of people to reach the
30. shores of America around 1000 A.D. However the main credit for the discovery of America goes to Christopher Columbus in the years around 1500 A.D.

9.

Columbus said about one of his voyages to the Americas,
"For nine days I was as one lost, without hope of life. Eyes never
35. beheld the sea so angry, so high, so covered with foam. The wind
not only prevented our progress, but offered no opportunity to run
behind any headland for shelter; hence we were forced to keep out
in this bloody ocean, seething like a pot on a hot fire. Never
did the sky look more terrible; for one whole day and night it
40. blazed like a furnace, and the lightning broke with
such violence."

The history of man's exploration of the Earth has spanned over
5000 years but the questions are, "What is there left to find out ?
Are there parts of the universe still to be explored ?" Now that we
45. have jet-powered aircraft, nuclear power, rocket-powered space
ships and high-tech submarines that can explore every land and sea
area of the world, it has become easier for man to go to previously
unknown places on earth and in space.

There are, however, vast stretches on the Earth and under the
50. oceans that lie unexplored. Mysteries still remain in the
impenetrable jungles of the Amazon Basin. Strange people,
animals and plants have been reported from the 3 million square
miles of forests on the borders of Russia and China. The trackless
wastes of the Polar regions are still shown as blank spaces on the
55. latest maps. Enormous parts of Africa, Australia and Siberia are
still virtually unexplored.

43. The words used to describe the unexplored Amazon Basin and the
Polar regions are

A.   strange and vast   B.   blank and virtually
C.   trackless and impenetrable   D.   million and borders
E.   latest and enormous

44. What was the main purpose of the earliest human explorers ?

A.   curiosity and safety   B.   find food and provide shelter
C.   survival and protection   D.   finding animals and rivers
E.   creating civilisation

45. Who described the ocean **"like a pot on a hot fire"** ?

A.   the Vikings   B.   the Egyptians
C.   the Minoan tribe   D.   the Romans
E.   Columbus

46. The **"amazing journey "** by an Egyptian 4000 years ago was to

A. Somaliland   B. Carthaginian
C. the Atlantic   D. the Mediterranean
E. America

47. Who followed the Phoenicians in the exploration of the Atlantic ?

A. the Minoans   B. the Russians
C. the Chinese   D. the Carthaginians
E. the Egyptians

48. On the borders of Russia and China there are

A. vast stretches of ocean and forests.
B. trackless wastes and blank spaces.
C. high, angry seas covered with foam.
D. blazing skies and lightning.
E. millions of square miles of forests.

49. The first group of people that are said to have reached the American shores were

A. the Carthaginians.   B. the Romans
C. the Vikings   D. the Chinese
E. Columbus and his followers.

50. From which country did the Phoenicians come ?

A. China   B. America   C. Greece
D. Lebanon   E. Europe

51. Columbus said the condition that stopped him from making progress on his voyages was

A. the angry sea   B. the wind
C. the bloody ocean   D. the pot of hot fire
E. the furnace

11.

52.	What has helped exploration in recent times ?

A.	Maps and charts of all the countries of the world.
B.	The invention of satellite navigation.
C.	The achievements of early explorers.
D.	The invention of rocket, jet and nuclear-powered machines.
E.	The introduction of modern sea-going vessels.

53.	What is meant by the expression, **"seething like a pot on a hot fire"** in **line 38** ?

A.	...boiling water in a saucepan over the fire.
B.	...agitated like a pot of boiling water.
C.	...calm and even like water in a hot pot.
D.	...hot, bubbling lava from a volcano.
E.	...terrible sky, blazing like a furnace.

54.	The word **"impenetrable"** in **line 51** means

A.	being secure	B.	well-cultivated
C.	explored and civilised	D.	unable to enter
E.	unable to disturb

55.	There are **three verbs** in **line 36**. These verbs are

A.	only, progress, but	B.	run, opportunity, our
C.	prevented, offered, run	D.	not, but, to
E.	only, progress, opportunity

General Section
To answer these questions, you may have to think about the passages you have read. Look back at these if you need to. Look also at the Index and Glossary.

56.	(a)	The VEGETABLE PLOT, MARY JANE IGNORED and CURIOUS EXPLORERS are in Capital letters because

A.	they are titles of passages.
B.	they have to stand out on the page.
C.	they are more easily identified.
D.	they need to be spelt properly.

(b). The words **burden**, **nutrients** and **fascination** in the GLOSSARY
      are

A. pronouns   B. adverbs
C. nouns   D. adjectives

57. (a) Which section of this test contains historical information ?

A. MARY JANE IGNORED   B. THE VEGETABLE PLOT
C. the GLOSSARY   D. CURIOUS EXPLORERS

(b). In which section of the test would you find a list of vegetables ?

A. the INDEX   B. THE VEGETABLE PLOT
C. the GLOSSARY   D. CURIOUS EXPLORERS

58. (a) The TWO words from the INDEX that are people's names are

A. Frank Trench / Christoper Columbus
B. Mary Jane Ignored / Somaliland
C. Amazon Basin / Mediterranean Sea
D. Phoenicians / Brooklyn

(b). The pair of words below which are the Group Names
      (Collective Nouns) for insects is

A. pack / gang   B. swarm / plague
C. nest / litter   D. flock / herd

59. (a) The best description of a magazine is

A. ..a booklet promoting a product or a service.
B. ..a record of daily events, appointments, observations.
C. ..a book containing facts about many subjects.
D. ..a monthly or weekly publication with articles by various writers.

13.

(b).   The **grammatically correct** statement below is

A.   Mary was the biggest of the twins.
B.   We hope the best of the two players wins the final.
C.   John picked up the thinner end of the rope.
D.   In Winter we have the worse weather of the year.

60.   (a)   The correct use of the **Past Tense** is in

A.   Yesterday John seen his friend crossing the road.
B.   The teacher had took his class to the swimming pool.
C.   Mary was given a bicycle for her birthday.
D.   Harry had spoke angrily to his sister.

(b).   The correct simile is

A.   ...as green as a frog.   B.   ...as swift as a hawk.
C.   ...as busy as a cat.   D.   ...as gentle as a swan.

GLOSSARY

hazardous----- dangerous
burden--------- load, weight, responsibility
economic------ financial, commercial
mammoth----- enormous, huge, very big
Hire Shop----- a shop from which you can rent machinery
rotavator------ a machine for digging
meagre-------- very little, inadequate, slight amount
nutrients------ substances that help health
trepidation--- worry, anxiety, fear
vessel--------- a container or a ship
precarious---- dangerous, insecure
courteous----- good-mannered, polite, respectful
gangplank---- portable bridge to get on or off ships
fascination--- attraction, charm, magic
hoisted------- lifted, raised up, elevated
embarked---- boarded ship
environment- surroundings, habitat
furnace------- closed chamber with a very hot fire

INDEX